Flips and Spins

Jill McDougall

Contents

Fit and Strong	2
Flips and Spins	4
Doing Gymnastics	8
How to Do a Forward Roll	12
Match It Up!	14
Index	16

Fit and Strong

It is fun to see gymnastics.

But gymnastics is also a fun sport to try.

rings

You can twist on bars and rings.

You can jump onto a beam.

beam

You can jump over a horse.

horse

Flips and Spins

This girl can do a handstand on the bar.

She can flip off the bar.

Then, she grabs the other bar.

This man can twist and spin up in the air. He can swing around a bar.

Then he can flip to the floor.

bar

7

Doing Gymnastics

Some boys and girls go to gymnastics class. Katie is learning how to spring and jump.

board

She **springs** off the board.

She **lands** on the mat!

Jake is learning the rings.

He **pulls** himself up.

rings

His arms will get strong.

How to Do a Forward Roll

1. Tuck your head under.

2. Roll over on your back.

3. Start to sit up.

4. Finish on your toes with your back straight. Well done!

Match It Up!

Look at these gymnastics moves. Match the moves to the correct photos.

handstand

cartwheel

headstand

starjump

Can you do any of these fun moves?

Turn to page 16 for the answers

15

Index

bars   2, 4–5, 6–7

beam   3

board   8–9

forward roll   12–13

horse   3

rings   2, 10–11

Match It Up Answers

starjump

cartwheel

handstand

headstand